CHRISTIAN

BY JASON BRICKWEG

BELLWETHER MEDIA • MINNEAPOLIS, MN

Are you ready to take it to the extreme? Torque books thrust you into the action-packed world of sports, vehicles, mystery, and adventure. These books may include dirt, smoke, fire, and dangerous stunts. WARNING: read at your own risk.

Library of Congress Cataloging-in-Publication Data

Brickweg, Jason.
 Christian / by Jason Brickweg.
   p. cm. -- (Torque: Pro wrestling champions)
 Includes bibliographical references and index.
 Summary: "Engaging images accompany information about Christian. The combination of high-interest subject matter and light text is intended for students in grades 3 through 7"--Provided by publisher.
   ISBN 978-1-60014-903-0 (hardcover : alk. paper)
 1. Christian, 1973---Juvenile literature. 2. Wrestlers--United States--Biography--Juvenile literature. I. Title.
  GV1196.C57B75 2013
  796.812092--dc23
  [B]
                                                      2012041210

This edition first published in 2013 by Bellwether Media, Inc.

No part of this publication may be reproduced in whole or in part without written permission of the publisher. For information regarding permission, write to Bellwether Media, Inc., Attention: Permissions Department, 5357 Penn Avenue South, Minneapolis, MN 55419.

Text copyright © 2013 by Bellwether Media, Inc. TORQUE and associated logos are trademarks and/or registered trademarks of Bellwether Media, Inc.

SCHOLASTIC, CHILDREN'S PRESS, and associated logos are trademarks and/or registered trademarks of Scholastic Inc.

Printed in the United States of America, North Mankato, MN.

The images in this book are reproduced through the courtesy of: Devin Chen, front cover, pp. 4, 6, 8, 9, 14-15, 16-17, 18-19, 20-21; Getty Images, pp. 4-5; Alamy, p. 10; Newscom, pp. 11, 12-13, 18.

CONTENTS

GRAND SLAM CHAMPION.... 4

WHO IS CHRISTIAN?............... 8

BECOMING A CHAMPION...... 16

GLOSSARY.................................. 22

TO LEARN MORE..................... 23

INDEX... 24

WARNING!

The wrestling moves used in this book are performed by professionals. Do not attempt to reenact any of the moves performed in this book.

GRAND SLAM CHAMPION

The World Heavyweight Championship was up for grabs at Extreme Rules 2011. It was halfway through the match when Christian made a big move. He used a **backdrop** to throw Alberto Del Rio onto a ladder. The **ladder match** was heating up!

ALBERTO DEL RIO

Wrestling Name:	Christian
Real Name:	William Jason Reso
Height:	6 feet, 1 inch (1.9 meters)
Weight:	212 pounds (96 kilograms)
Started Wrestling:	1995
Finishing Move:	Killswitch

Del Rio and Christian battled back and forth. Del Rio delivered his **Enzuigiri** to Christian's head. Christian performed a **Spear**. Suddenly Brodus Clay interfered. It looked like Del Rio had the win. Then Edge showed up to distract him. Christian knocked Del Rio off the ladder. He grabbed the title and became a **Grand Slam Champion**!

WHO IS CHRISTIAN?

William Jason Reso was born on November 30, 1973 in Ontario, Canada. As a child, he spent a lot of time playing hockey. He and his best friend, Adam Copeland, were big wrestling fans.

At age eighteen, Copeland wrote an essay about why he wanted to become a wrestler. He entered it in a contest and won. The prize was free training at Sully's Gym in Toronto. Reso later followed Copeland to Sully's.

Reso started wrestling in the Canadian **independent circuit** in 1995. He won titles on his own and with Copeland. The two wrestled as a **tag team** called High Impact.

In 1998, Reso was invited to a World Wrestling Entertainment (WWE) training camp. Copeland had recently joined WWE and recommended Reso. WWE signed Reso after he finished training.

QUICK HIT!

Early on, Reso wrestled as Christian Cage. This ring name combined the names of famous actors Christian Slater and Nicolas Cage.

Reso **debuted** in WWE as Christian. He joined up with Copeland, called Edge, and Gangrel. The three wrestled as The Brood for about a year. Christian and Edge then wrestled as a tag team for the next few years. They won seven World Tag Team Championships.

QUICK HIT!

Christian and Edge had ongoing feuds with the Hardy Boyz and the Dudley Boyz.

BECOMING A CHAMPION

In 2001, Christian and Edge parted ways. Christian formed other **alliances** and chased singles titles. He captured the Intercontinental Championship three times.

Christian left WWE in 2005 to wrestle for Total Nonstop Action Wrestling. After several years, he returned to WWE. In 2011, Christian won the World Heavyweight Championship for the first time. He claimed his fourth Intercontinental Championship a year later.

QUICK HIT!
WWE cast Christian as a cocky villain for a time. He called himself Captain Charisma.

Christian has used many different moves in the ring. His **signature moves** include the Frog Splash and the Tornado DDT. The Frog Splash is a frog-like leap from the top rope. For the Tornado DDT, Christian climbs the ropes and grabs his opponent's head. Then he swings around in midair and falls backward with his opponent.

FROG SPLASH

Christian often uses the Killswitch to end a match. First he grabs his opponent's arms. Then he twists him around and brings him to the ground. This is one **finishing move** that has set Christian up for many championship pins!

QUICK HIT!

Christian also uses the Spear as a finishing move. He does it to honor Edge.

GLOSSARY

alliances—partnerships or united groups

backdrop—a move in which a wrestler lifts a charging opponent over his head and then drops him behind his back

debuted—first appeared

Enzuigiri—a move in which a wrestler jumps up and kicks the back of his opponent's head

finishing move—a wrestling move meant to finish off an opponent so that he can be pinned

Grand Slam Champion—a professional wrestler who has won four different WWE championships

independent circuit—the minor league of professional wrestling

ladder match—a wrestling match in which a wrestler must climb a ladder to claim the belt or briefcase at the top

signature moves—moves that a wrestler is famous for performing

Spear—a move in which a wrestler charges and dives at a standing opponent, driving his shoulder into the opponent's stomach

tag team—two wrestlers who compete as a team

TO LEARN MORE

AT THE LIBRARY
Black, Jake. *The Ultimate Guide to WWE*. New York, N.Y.: Grosset & Dunlap, 2011.

Price, Sean Stewart. *The Kids' Guide to Pro Wrestling*. Mankato, Minn.: Edge Books, 2012.

Stone, Adam. *Edge*. Minneapolis, Minn.: Bellwether Media, Inc., 2012.

ON THE WEB
Learning more about Christian is as easy as 1, 2, 3.

1. Go to www.factsurfer.com.

2. Enter "Christian" into the search box.

3. Click the "Surf" button and you will see a list of related Web sites.

With factsurfer.com, finding more information is just a click away.

INDEX

Alberto Del Rio, 4, 7
backdrop, 4
Brodus Clay, 7
Canada, 9, 10
Canadian independent circuit, 12
Copeland, Adam, 9, 10, 12, 14
debut, 14
Edge, 7, 14, 16, 21
Enzuigiri, 7
Extreme Rules, 4
feuds, 14
finishing move, 7, 20, 21
Frog Splash, 19
Gangrel, 14
Grand Slam Champion, 7
High Impact, 12
hockey, 9
Intercontinental Championship, 16
Killswitch, 7, 21
ladder match, 4, 7
ring names, 12, 16
signature moves, 19
Spear, 7, 20, 21
tag team, 12, 14
The Brood, 14
Tornado DDT, 19
Total Nonstop Action Wrestling, 16
training, 10, 12
World Heavyweight Championship, 4, 16
World Tag Team Championship, 14
World Wrestling Entertainment (WWE), 12, 14, 16